OWL WOES: A POETRY COLLECTION

BY: FELICIA RENEA

FOR WOMEN

BURN

Flames flicker
Embers travel
Set fire to redwood
The home we built
Now fills with smoke
Choking on broken promises
Wooden home built with hands
Built with love
Set fire so quickly
So easily
When it stops burning,
I hope you remember me

RAGE

Bottled in jars
That are stacked high to the ceiling
Jars that are tightly shut
They are ready to explode
Heart beats faster
Ready to implode
Metal bat breaks jars
Screaming glass
Sharp cut shards
Bottles of rage
Anger releasing
Releasing every moment
I remember

FEMININE

You ask for femininity
What does that even mean?
A warrior with blades
A flower crown beauty
We can be all these things
Mothers can make the world go 'round
And if that is not my desire
My hands will not be bound
Life starts through us
Mother earth carries
Protect our flowers
We must

FATALE

Femme fatale
Wooden dowels
Stakes in the ground
Fire starts
Rip her apart
She dances in the moonlight
As flames grow higher
Wolves howl
Femme fatale

MEDUSA

One snake, two snake, three snake
Four
Medusa's head rolled on to the floor
All she wanted was to turn you to stone
To watch you crumble
To do to you what you did to her heart
Break you into a million pieces
Just as you did to her soul
No longer alive
No pain anymore

DEMONS

I do not fear my demons
I conquered them a long time ago
They haunted my dreams
Hiding in the shadows
Stood over my bed
They made my heart rattle
They tried to shame me with my mistakes
And cage me in my past
Look at your scars
I did not listen
I broke through the bars
I smudged them away
They tried to push me around
My demons fear me now

BLACK TAR

I once was clean
But then I fell into black tar
Streams slowly pulling me under
Quicksand dreams
I have failed
Is that what this means
For so long,
I begged to be put out of my misery
Sinking lower
I was hoping people would forget me
There I was
Melting
When it started to rain
Quick sand disappearing
Ridding black tar pain
I rose from the deep depth craters
Hurt shattered
Bright big flaming star
For once,
I did matter

SLIVER

I want to live within the shadows of your soul

Deep dark crevices
Slivers of touching light
Making spirit whole

SUCCUBUS

Man eating
Psychotic tendencies
You no longer mean that much to me
I want to rip you apart
From the inside out
Devouring your heart
Then spitting it back out
Blood runs dry
Stained carpets are soaked
It was you
I wanted you the most
Soul sucked us
Watch out for her
Succubus

I AM MOTHER

I am in the soil and the trees
The vines where grapes grow
I am the fall colored leaves
I am the lighting that strikes down on open farms
The tornados that sound the alarm
The green grass that grows from the soil
Vegetables you cut to boil
I grew from the ground
Rain and hurricanes
I am everywhere and around
Snowflakes
The sky and the clouds
Gripping tree limbs
Swaying in the wind
I am not this, that or the other
There can only be one
I am mother

DROWNING

You are drowning in the deepest parts of the ocean
No one even notices
Air bubble float at the surface
Until disappeared, no more
You can do laps
Even float on your back
People will say,
“see, she knows how to swim, see, she is okay”
Stay at the surface
Stay close to the shore
Keep your head above water
They do not notice
No one even bothers

SIRENS

I hear your songs calling to me
I yearned to find
Stormy seas
You heard my hearts rhythm
Behind rocks, waiting in the waters
A danger to bother
I hear you
I hear your song
Like sirens in the street
Siren songs in the middle of the ocean
You wait for me,
To come to you
No more
No motion

POET

I fell in love with a poet
Her words,
Wrapped around me
Like a python securing its prey
I was mesmerized by her voice
How could she make me feel this way?
She punctured my heart
Ink filling up the chambers
I could not have her
I only had her words
Ventricles of anger
Every word she wrote
I felt each loop
Each scribble
The pain consumed my body
She hides hers
She does not show it
Pens with no ink
I fell in love with a poet

DARKNESS

Falling from clouds
Misty travels
Ripping wings
Blacktop ground
The fall was hard
All light had refused to shine for you
Sunshine beacon refusing to flare
Exiled from the light
Broken limbs and body weakened
Crawling through blacked out sidewalks
Moonlight arriving to hold your hand
Shining a path
Guiding you through the darkness

INTRUSIVE

Inner dialogue, like whirlpools of words
Words swallowed by ocean waves
Intrusive hurricane awakenings
Nerve shocks in my brain
Like lighting storms
Connecting spinal cords
To the main frame
Heart beating
Blood vessels going dry
Supply me
Cardiac arrest
Locked in my mind

PTSD

Reflections of the past
Past life regressions
Who am I anymore?
There are thoughts to never mention
Triggers pulled
Buttons pushed
Trauma flashes
Sleepless nights
Nightmares awaken
I am screaming again
PTSD shaken

IMPATIENT

Induced
Wire snaps
Reduced
Open mail
On the table
No longer waiting
Impatient

IMPULSIVE

I grab items at the store
Throw it in the basket
Price, do not ask it
These things from the store end up on the wall
Shattered
I am repulsive
Without thinking
Action
impulsive

UNSTABLE

Table leg wobble
Loose
Unsteady
Hands dirty
Elbows off
Sway
Unfixed
Unable
No screws
Unstable

MESSY ME

Excuse me
I was not honest
My mind is still a mess
When you asked how I was doing
I wish there was more I had said
I am sorry
I would not let you see
I did not show you the truth
Oh, messy me

TRIGGERED

Nails on a chalkboard
Screeching
You pressed my buttons
I am seething
Leave me to wallow
In my self pity
Grave digger
Gritty
Aimed triggered

HYPERVENTILATING

Hyperventilating
As the voices are screaming
I cover my ears
I cannot breathe
You may hate me,
That is true
But you will never hate me more than I do

I AM NOT OKAY

Pure honesty
Pure dread
Full of fear that you will judge me
I am messed up in the head
I wish I could tell you that I am always fine
It is not the truth
I am lying
I have low lows
High highs
I look you in the face
And tell you I am fine
But I really am
On most days
On the others
I am not okay

INSOMNIA

Creeping ideations
Word vomit in my brain
Letters form like creations
So long, I have been locked inside my mind
Days on end
Spit fire of screaming matches
Negative thoughts dancing together
Weaknesses and ideas
Biting my nails
The light fights to see us
On insomnia nights,
When I feel at my worst
I do not believe in myself
A rough wreck
I still lay my head down
I still make sure to get my rest

SLEEPLESS

I tossed and turned
I ached and groaned
You were snoring
I felt so alone
Looking up at a dark ceiling
Moonlight shines through the room
On sleepless nights I remember
I will always have the moon

GRINDING

Fall asleep so deeply
Into the abyss of anxiety
Stress from the day
Future in the way
I am my own worst enemy
If my soul never returned,
Would you remember me?
Down
Down
Unwinding
It is all in my mind
Late night teeth grinding

DREAMER

I dream and dream
Looking for answers and meaning
I am left disappointed
I am reaping
Images
Scenarios
What is it that I am not seeing?
I cannot see her face
I see her
Deep sleep wanderer
Forever a dreamer

SHADOWS

Shadows dancing at moon light hours
Open windows with slivers of brightness
Darkness as tall as castle towers
I walk through unlit sidewalks
Through black masses
Behind me,
My shadow dances

VELVET

Crescent moon
Bright auras
Sleeping skies
No promise of tomorrow
Glowing
Wrapped in shiny stars
Black velvet
Never complaining
As the world is constantly turning
Lonely nights
Flames burning

RAVEN

Raven caw's
Owls who
In the night I search for you
You are a constellation
A dead star creation
Older than time and space
Never new
Meteors shoot across
Raven winged skies
As I wait for you

SLITHER

Serpent slides
Scales dry
Shedding skin
A new beginning
Start of sin
In tall grass
Slither in

FELIS CATUS

Cat scratches
Scratching tree tower
Furniture strings hang
You never see them do it
No one to blame
Cat scratch fever
Left with no name
Zoomies across the room
Always waking us
Purr love
Felis catus

INK

Hieroglyphics in pyramids
Carvings in rocks
The art left behind
Forever capsuled in time
The ink I wear
Is the art for my body
Message to sender
Death deteriorates
I will not live forever

HEARSE

No belts to buckle
This is your last ride
No body in the casket
Only your heart died
A driver and a hearse
People stare
Spirit spared
My soul will forever stay

CASTLE RUINS

Sinking swamp bayou
Slow streams
Leading to castle ruins
Empty and abandoned
Old roots suffocations
Opened windows
That once let light in
Breakthrough sunshine no more
How did a castle end up here?
Alone
Desolate
In ruins

GHOST

I feel you in the air that I breathe
As the wind wraps around me
Holding
Holding on to your presence
Forever gone
Memories we once had
Forever cemented
A ghost in my mind
No longer existing
Lost in time

PLAGUE

Innocence
Taken
Plaguing my brain
Infecting my arteries
Infecting my veins
Creating a plague that made me insane
My heart exploded
Black blood aneurysm
Flooding my insides
Pulling my hair out
Blood shot red eyes

TOMBSTONE

She walks through the cemetery
Floating through tombstones
She remembers his face
Year after year
Same time, same place
Same month, same day
He visits
An anniversary of lost love
He brings flowers
She screams his name, but he does not hear a sound

I AM HERE

Right in front of you
Her name carved in stone
He leaves
She is left all alone
Amongst the tombstones
She cries
He never stays
I never said goodbye

WEBS

Cobweb lies sway in corners of the room
A maze of words glistens as it touches the light
Arachnid abandonment
Sewing labyrinth screams
A beautiful design that was once home
Empty hallways
Only cobwebs stay
Caught by the wind and let go
Until then
I sit in the dark
As my whispers echo

GUILLOTINE

Like Marie at the guillotine...
I just want to be seen...
End the misery....

MIRRORS

Small mirrors
Tall mirrors
Round mirrors
Square mirrors
Hang on to flame lit hallways
Candlelight tears
Covered by sheets
I cannot stand to see me

Please do not remove the veils
They protect me
My energy
Soul sucked
Entity

GLASS HOUSE

Throw sticks
Stones
Bricks

The glass house you live in is thin

Keep throwing your junk
It lives at the roots
My glass house
Is bulletproof

GLASS

Bricks thrown
Glass shatters

Front wall window
You locked the front door
Why couldn't you just let me in?

WRAPPED

Wrapped my wrist
Medical supplies
Epidermis
Membrane exposed
Tape my mouth closed
Nobody knows

BLADE

Do me a favor
Take the knife out of my back
You know,
The one you put there
Stuck
Intact
The blade
You used on my skin
When I did not give up
I did not let you win

SAND

I am the last sand in the hourglass
I fall gently on dunes
The glass is empty
We are all doomed
There was nothing left to fill
There was not enough room
Did we turn too quickly?
Did we turn too soon?
As I lay supine
I remember the time we wasted
The warning signs

SUFFOCATING

Hit man hired
Plastic bag over face
I cannot breathe
I am suffocating
Release me this once
Oxygen fills my lungs
You never let go
Blue lips frost bite
Falling to the floor
There is no more fight

SOUL MATE

Rotate
Soul mate
First sight?
Yeah right
Listen to your head
Never your heart
Love does not exist
No start

HAZEL

Honey eyes
Sunset rays of sunshine
Everchanging
Green as the grass
Back and forth
Black in wrath
Brown like stump roots underground
Like honey for tea
The changing colors of autumn leaves
Caramel green apple haze
Calm hazel eyes
Full of rage

SCORPIO MAN

Scorpio man
Wearing a black tie suit
Raining in dark clouds
Dark seas of blue
He is a mystery
My muse
Will not speak unless spoken to
Pluto no longer in the system
The universe engulfs them
Intuition high
Like waves of the ocean
Hades robes
Dances on firestones
Will not walk in crowds
They are better alone
Intimidating passion
Seeing red in reactions
Mysteriously consuming
Curiosity eats at you
Obsessed with the unknowing
A Scorpio man built from the shadows
Night sky roaming

CAUGHT

Candlelight, embers
The night our souls connected
I remember
Bright eyes
With excitement and wonder
Night skies
You held me close
Warm hands
Hands over the candle flame
You left it there
Too close
Too long
Hands caught fire third degree burns
You wrapped them up
It was unheard of
I wanted it out
I wanted to blow the candle out
You insisted it stayed lit
With tears in our eyes
Yours from the pain
We kept the flame going
Minds insane

DECADES

You ask, "what are we?"
Innocent eyes with wild hearts
The start,
Of a heartbreaking ending
Onion layers peeled back
Year after year
I shed
I am pieces apart
Insides slowly bulging into open air
You begged to pull back ribs
You sought, a beating heart
A decade later
You got what you wanted
You did not like what you saw
The real me
How tables have turned
I ask, "what are we?"

SAILOR

Sailor, working in the deepest parts of the sea
The deepest parts of the oceans
Working endlessly
Sun shines
Black outs
No human contact for weeks
Stars in the night sky
Sirens with black eyes
The seas call to you
My heart breaks to have you here
Weeks and weeks pass
You do not hear the songs I sing
My tears I cry
I beg the sea to bring you back to me
Again, you sail away
The waters have your heart
My heart in your hands
Stay

BURNS

Matchbox lies
You lit the match
Threw it at my feet
Bursting into flames
I did not cry or scream
I accepted my fate
Flames and flesh
Unrecoverable burns
Unrecoverable pain
An unrecognizable face
It was the last thing I saw
A smile of deceit
On that dark night
When you lit the match at my feet

DEVIL

The devil courted me
We danced through the night
He bought me red roses
He poured me red wine
He held me in his arms
As I was uncontrollably weeping
He laid me next to ocean waves
As I am soundly sleeping
I was not scared
I have faced evil before
His claws scratched my head
Soothing scalp
I was not worried about him at all
It was the wolves in sheep's clothing
The ones praying I would fall

BONES

I buried you in the backyard
Your body decomposed
Liquid heart
A pile of bones
Mandible lies
Eye socket caves of nothingness
Where tears once dried
Your bones in a bag
Piled in the bed where we once laid
Anatomy class display
Spinal latch
Bone marrow biopsy
We were not a match

SPICY

You say I have an attitude
You call me spicy
You are overthinking
Overreacting
Tread lightly
Like salsa on food
You crave the heat
When it is too spicy
You decide it is too much for me

CURSE

I thought I wanted to be a nurse
Dreams change
I was supposed to mend this curse
Healing hands
Unable to heal a broken heart
Broken families
Curse never lifted
World ripped apart

SAD CLOWN

You were dancing in the streets
Clapping hands
Tapping feet
The crowd joined you
Staying in your rhythm
Clown makeup painted on your face
All they could see was the smile you drew
Not the smeared under eyes
Tears once new
Pin drops
No sound
Sad clown

INFECTION

Icy cold
In comparison
To my black heart
Like an infection
The bubonic plague
Rat trap trays
Sticky feet
On egg shells we walk
Infecting my veins
My black heart

HAUNTED

Dimensions crossed
You lost
Spirit weeping
Forever grieving
Haunted by the ghost of you
Love has no meaning

ICE

Dry ice
Sealed shut
Dare to touch it
You will not feel a thing
An icy heart
Where no songs sing

HURT

You can heal from a broken arm
Maybe not a broken spine
But...
What can heal the inside?
Emotions
Moods
The trauma brews
Paint splattered
On white shirts
It no longer hurts

REWIND

It was not all bad
If you rewind…….
There it is……
The good times.

BLACK WIDOW

In corners of the room
Black widow waiting
She is coming for you
She sings you a lullaby
She puts you to sleep
Fangs in your skin
Arachnophobia
Sewed and reaped

EYES SEWED SHUT

Needle push pins
Threaded lies
Tired of tears
Careless cry
Butterfly stitch
Shut eyes

EYES WIDE OPEN

Eyes wide open
I see everything
Ophthalmic speculum
Speculation
You do not know me at all
Vampire invitation
Blood runs deep
No relations

DIVINE

Light work intervention
Divine inception
Clouds carry
Next lesson
Astronomers
Science inventions
Wormhole recollections
Confidential
No mentions
Forever bound
Soul retention
Divine contracts
Reality in session

ROAM

My soul is searching for a home
In the trees
Where forests sit lonely
The secrets they possess
Deeper
The darkness seems homely
Not in people
Not in places
Trails unknown
Galaxies
Between stars
I am still looking
I still roam

OMEN

Take in the word
This is not a sermon
Life is happening
Take in the moment
No good things ahead
This is an omen

PIECES

Empty puzzle
Never finished
Never whole
Puzzle pieces missing
Are the pieces that you stole
It just sits there
Uncompleted
Forever missing
Jigsaw defeated

BURNOUT

Over work
Over work
Here's overtime
Take it
Whine
Cry
More wine
More and more
Work
Foaming at the mouth
Burn out

TUMOR

Mass
A tumor
Sticky insides
Brain fluid
Rumors
Malignant
Benign
Infecting me
No more time

EYES

Step in their shoes
Look through their eyes
Through optical lenses
Disgusting memories of lies
You poke the bear
You poke and pry
You wonder why
I stay away
You wonder why
I want you to...
Stay out of my life

LOST

When I think of the days when I would walk alone
On highways
Judgement and betrayal
I was lost
There was nothing I could say
Best foot forward
Sidewalk step off
Tempted by headlights
Hypnotizing
Attempted
No one wanted me around
Brakes screeching
I just wanted to be found

ALONE

Dial up phone
Ringtones
I keep the phone off the hook
No one calls anyway
I am never coming home
In my own little world
Forever alone

WICKED

Good and evil
Light and dark
No wrongs
No rights
No one to fix it
We are our own worst enemies
People are wicked

REMEMBER

Oh, I remember
Forgive
Never forget
I hold no grudges
But no one has apologized yet

CAGE

You put me here,
Deadbolted shut
Behind bars
Stuck
Let me out
Let me run
I no longer belong to you
Cage me
I will get through

FIREWORKS

Monsters are real
The world is filled with evil
Firework explosions
Canvas or easel
Painting across the sky
Sparks
Sparkles
Colors array
Leave the art to the artist
Fireworks to ward the bad away

LAVA

Volcanic smoke filled the air
I could finally breathe again
I walked through
As lava surrounded at my feet
Its warmth
Engulfing me
Carrying me to the top
Dropping me down in heat bubbles
I swam
Never melting me to the bone
I lay on my back
Looking up at the ashy sky
For once,
I did not want to die

HEAT

Let me choke you until you are unconscious
Come back for remembrance
Tight grip, do you feel my vengeance?
Can you feel the anger
The heat from my hands
The moment I stopped caring
Blacked out
Moments I could not understand

RISEN

Falling into flames
I was to perish
Billowing smoke
Consuming lungs
Inhalation
No recollection
I was birthed in the fire
Triangular prism
I could not be contained
I have risen

FLAMES

Paper hearts rained down from the sky
Like uncontrollable tears from a human eye
Floating down slowly
Burning to ash
Engulfed in a fire that was already started
Flames dancing below them

JITTERS

Coffee bean
Giving jitters
Espresso shot
Hands shiver
Medium roast
Dark roast
Hands shake
Heart pounds
Café latte
Only fresh when ground

ALARM

Alarm system steady
Buttons pressed
Ready
Locked down
No longer welcomed
Siren's sound

OIL

Drop oil into milk
Separate
Split
Drip down
Ground
Soaked and slipped
Oil stains
Left behind
Residue
Over time

SUNSET

Pinks
Purples
Sky haze
Daylight ending its day
The moon rotating in
Lighting the way

LIGHTNING

Lightning strikes
Dry deserts
Fetal position
Hands over my head
Hail inquisitions
Thor thundering
Shocks uttering
Lightning bolts
Charges
There is no more energy
Striking down
Fire alignments
Erratically electric
Take in the moment

ASTEROID

Hurling through space and time
An asteroid on its way
So I can meet my demise
It may hit earth
But it will land directly on me
Screaming
Shouting
No time to run out
I wish an asteroid was on its way
So I do not have to confront,
The words I will never say

MARS

Perseverance
Traveling to mars
Headstrong
Deployed amongst the stars
Traveling alone
Red planet envy
Destined to roam
Fourth planet from the sun
Iron oxide dust
Not rotten
Not rust
God of war landing
Earth was not enough

ROOTS

Photosynthesis beginnings
Planted seed in the ground
Roots began to grow

Pipe bursting sounds
Deeper and deeper
Roots moving through soil
Blood is thicker than water
So they say
What about oil
What happens to the trees
Termite ridden
Tsunami debris
Chopped down,
But the roots stay underneath
Forgotten
No longer needed
Making room
To plant new seeds

GOLDEN STATE

Where the poppies grow
The sun shines
Sand between toes
California heat
Bare feet
The place that raised me
Earthquakes
Mountain curve
Golden state

AFTERSHOCK

California native
San Andreas fault line hollow
It is not the earthquakes you should be afraid of
It is the aftershocks that follow

PINES

Pine trees
Connecting
Earthling
I am being
Space and time
In a moment
Rhythms and rhymes
I am still
In the pines

FLOWERS

Sunflowers and daisies
Seasonal allergies
Eyes hazy
Pollen travels to attack my sinuses
Flowers and trees
They always seem to find me
Chasing me down to cause me misery
Summer and spring
Hay fever overcomes me
Laying in grass
Red nose and puffy eyes
It is all that I know
It is mine

HEAL

Open wound
Made by harsh remarks
Deeper and deeper
You throw in the salt
Epidermis layers
I am screaming
You were never going to change
I stitch my own wound
I heal my own pain

FLIGHTLESS

An owl without wings
How absurd
Scapula holes
You can see the wing bone
Healed where they ripped
Where feathers once shed
Growing no more
Torn from her flesh
From hungry wolves
Blood on their teeth
Feathers float
Lightness
An owl
Can never be flightless

NIGHT OWL

I am up at 2AM
Writing in blood
Giving you my heart in words
I am giving you everything
Metaphors
Vowels
Dark hour
Night owl

NEVER GIVE UP

Butterfly cocoons
Wrapped up
Blooming soon
Evolution takes time
Patience is key
Only I can believe in me
You still feel stuck
The universe is listening
Never give up

THE END

ABOUT THE AUTHOR

Felicia Renea is a self-published poetry writer. She was born in Santa Rosa, CA but currently resides in Washington state. She is Native American from the Big Valley Band of Pomo Indians. She was in fourth grade when she wrote her first poem. At the age of fourteen is when she started to use writing as a form of expression and finding that it was the only way to express how she was feeling. She hopes her poetry can bring inspiration and connection. Felicia wants others to know that they are not alone and to never give up.

Made in the USA
Thornton, CO
04/06/24 04:01:30

742f77b1-4155-4ed5-b863-2dd35ac22ca3R01